The Balladeers Present...

Glens an

GW01464127

Where the Lagan Flows

Lyrics for the album of the same title

INTRODUCTION

Welcome to 'Glens and Gantries,' the Balladeers' first publication and album. It is an attempt to tread new ground by combining song and poetry in one package.

Musically the album features a range of styles including Country Folk, Traditional Irish and Blues. With one exception (the Titanic), all pieces are original. The lyric book is divided into two sections; one for songs and the other for poetry. Not all the poems are featured on the album.

On a lyrical level we explore Northern life, past and present. Rural and city communities are examined against the back-drop of emigration, shipping disasters and the battle against alienation. Victorian gin-palaces feature heavily!

The Balladeers are a company of musicians, poets and storytellers with an orientation towards the community. They believe that there is much untapped talent in the North, more often than not in deprived areas. It would delight them to see a revival in folk consciousness and community self-expression. They oppose prejudice and sectarianism.

Glenn Simpson
North Belfast, Jan 1994

This album/anthology set has been sponsored by 'The Foundation for Sport and the Arts.' We extend our gratitude.

Special thanks: Ex-Isle (the Brussels based company of musicians and writers).
Hazelwood College.
The Front Page Bar.

Published by
Balladeers Press
c/o C C R C
Hazelwood College
70 Whitewell Road
Belfast
BT36 7ES
Tel: (0232) 779056

CONTRIBUTORS

Glenn Simpson: Production of album and
                                  lyric book. Songwriting,
                                  guitar and harmonica.

Bernard Conlon: Poetry and publicity.

Benny Adams: Songwriting, guitar and
                                  vocals.

Jim Johnston: Poetry and layout.

Marie O'Neill: Harp and songwriting.

Dermot Rooney: Songwriting, bottleneck
                                  guitar and dobro.

John McSorley: Artist.
                                  Original sketches.

Angela Rooney: Vocals.

John B McCabe: Poetry.

Anne Moreland: Vocals and songwriting.

Paul MacAree: Recording engineer.
                                  Production.

                                  Percussion and double
                                  bass.

Cover:
Workers leaving Harland & Wolff. The Titanic *can be
seen on the slip in the background.*

CONTENTS

SONGS

Bushmills Distillery

NOBODY LISTENS TO ME

They're flying them in from all 'round the world,
To shoot pictures of the places where the stones get hurled,
They photograph pavements, take pictures of the walls,
On the Shankill, Ballymurphy, Tigers Bay and The Falls.
The cameras pan, the shutters click,
'Round the burning van, as the smoke gets thick,
I'd like to tell them my story,
But I'm a poor boy, hate no-one, so nobody listens to me.

They root around for any signs,
Of confrontation, to fit the headlines,
When thousands march in unity,
It's just not deemed newsworthy.
When the sirens wail, the film whirls,
When someone shouts, or a flag unfurls,
They show what they want you to see,
And I'm a poor boy, hate no-one, so nobody listens to me.

To get images of hatred they're employed,
To please the editor of some tabloid,
A balanced view is just ignored,
Afraid their readers might get bored.
When the bullets fly, or a bomb explodes,
To get in all the shots, the cameraman reloads,
I'd give my views to them for free
But I'm a poor boy, hate no-one, so nobody listens to me.

YOUR SHIP IS MOORED

(FULLDUE STONE)

Big ship came sailing into the bay
Thunder and lightning on that dreadful day
And the big ship went down.
"The Carcass" she went down.

Villagers were watching and in their dismay
Ran for their tiny boats and rowed into the spray
But all hands went down.
All hands went down.

Mary Mc Cracken stood on the sands
Wearing a shawl and wringing her hands.
She was crying for her man.
Crying for her man.

When the storm subsided
The people in the Glens
Carried the coffins and buried their men.
Carried the coffins and buried their men.

Johnny MacCallister was laid to rest
Where the quiet brown water
Of the Dún touched his head.
The quiet brown water of the Dún caressed his head.

Mary McCracken could not be consoled
Her lover Johnny was eighteen years old.
Johnny "The Goat" was eighteen years old.

Later that night when the mourners had gone
Mary came for Johnny and slept on his gravestone.
Slept on his gravestone and never woke again.

Some words were found written on stone
"Your ship is moored, love, and you have come home."
Your ship is moored, love, and you have come home.

(Johnny MacCallister's resting-place can be found in the graveyard at Cushendún, Co. Antrim.)

BROWN STREAM OF SUMMER

Once again I'm in Glendún
Brown stream of summer gone.
A furtive knock upon your door
Then was a long, long embrace
Released you slowly, kissed your face.

And we went up to Glendún
Beneath the bridge towards the sun.
Stop, bend over, tie your shoe
You don't even know that I'm looking at you.

We go down to the river's edge
To the stream we made a pledge.
Sleeping now and the world surmising
All the time the river rising.

At dusk we walked to Cushendún
The boats were moored in Cushendún.
On the bridge you said to me
"Deep, deep eternity."
Brown stream of summer gone.
Once again I'm in Glendún.

Cushendún

10

ONE MORE BAR

Since you left me, I just haven't been right,
Can't concentrate, I lie awake half the night,
A complete cure is so hard to find,
I just can't seem to drink you out of my mind,
But if I cut through here, maybe one more bar and I'm free.

I want to escape, from this cold misery,
I get real drunk, but your face still haunts me,
I feel down in The Crown, and I was refused,
From the Washington, and even the Castle Mews,
But if I cut through here, maybe one more bar and I'm free.
In Morrisons and the Rotterdam, I drink to forget you,
By the time I'm told, that I gotta scram,
I can almost imagine that I never met you.

I fell off my stool, in The Liverpool,
Got kicked out of Pat's, for acting the fool.
From the Morning Star, I got slung out
And from the Front Page and Kitchen, after one pint of stout,
But if I cut through here maybe one more bar and I'm free.

Kelly's Cellars, then on to Lavery's
By the Duke of York, I'd wound up on my knees,
And though I was drunk, I tried to deduce,
If I was just using you, as a convenient excuse
But if I cut through here, maybe one more bar and I'm free.

KITTY

Kitty roared into the twenties Strand pocket nation
A tight community inbred parish under heel.
Severed education and then with Peg and Eileen
To Owen O'Cork and Greeves to wind and rove and reel.

Wed Tom wed sisterhood in secret opposition
To brethren select who tramp the grape and sup the wine.
Shallow voice rise on not an inch claims the measure
And simple truths well told forge a movement into line.

In wee man's company men of forties and fifties
Kitty roared again with serious intent.
No flower bull or posture this honest woman feared
For acidic tongue and venom a scrupulous imp.

Then little boys came of age interpretation lost
Conspiracy to purge the hard knocks from the block.
From secret eye to exile real warmth allowed to show
For family and friends still source of tender mock.

More might have recollected when their own lives diverged
Replenished a little of the sparks long ignite.
The final passing in stifled effacement
Celebrating God not life's spirited fight.

LOOK ELSEWHERE

Saturday night for this gingerbread girl
War paint scent and tribal clothes.
Bess just wants someone to take care of her
Setting her stall where Peter goes.

Recognition and then a smile
This fantasy from daily tedium.
Words exchanged for too short a while
She scrubs the floors he struts them.

Pete wants more of a challenge, a little less wear,
Bess takes it all in her stride.
He knows he'll score elsewhere
She knows she's past it at thirty-five.

The Poor House, Clifton Street.

Vulnerable woman seeks male company
The signal comes out clear.
Plenty of banter among the lonely
Nervous chat and stilted humour.

No panic yet no impulsive haste
Another hour of music is time enough.
This one is married, what a waste
His poor wife must be getting it rough.

Drink up please move to the front of the bar
Then tense negotiations are made.
You can't be choosy when you go to war
This married man is getting laid.

The Gate Lodge, Friar's Bush Graveyard,
Stranmillis Road.

SUN AND MOON

The sun has not gone down yet
And the moon's up in the sky,
Each one vying for attention,
Each one trying to catch my eye.
I don't know which one to look at,
I can't tell which way to turn,
I've confused, nothing is clear now,
I'll never learn.

He's been with me in the daytime
And his warmth is all around
But your light is shining on me
You don't have to make a sound.
I can't tell which one to follow
I don't know which way to go
I'm confused, nothing is clear now
I just don't know.

Well the moon is in ascension
And the sun is out of sight.
Am I heading into darkness?
Am I drifting into light?
I don't know which way I'm going.
I can't tell which way to turn.
I'll never learn, I'll never learn.

THIS ROAD

Dedicated to Julia Simpson

I was made on this road
Here I found my feet.
Stand beside the window
Look down on the street.

Chorus
*And this road it has no lock or key.
There are no Gods here.
There are no fools to waste my time
When I'm on... this road.*

The Hatfield Bar, Ormeau Road.

This road is older than the hills
An odyssey of miles.
And the moon shines on this road
A gas light in the sky.

Chorus

And this road it has no lock or key
There are no Gods here.
There are no fools to waste my time
When I'm on... this road.

Now you have to leave this road
Miles and miles behind.
As you walk away from this road
You look ... behind.

And you wonder why you stop and think
Why does a road make you stop and think?
Why don't you walk on a straight line?
Never look... behind.

I was made on this road
Here I found my feet.
Stand beside this window
Look down on the street.

Chorus
And this road it has no lock or key
There are no Gods here.
There are no fools to waste my time
When I'm on... this road.

WHERE THE LAGAN FLOWS

Where the shadows fall
In the night of no recall
I'm waiting for you.
Waiting patiently for you.

You're taking up my time
Always on my mind
An image of you
A photograph, a picture of you.

Once upon a time
When you were mine
Loving you.
Making love to you.

Chorus
Making love to you ...

Where the Lagan flows
I thought that love could grow
When I first kissed you.
Said a poem for you.

Still the river flows
The future no one knows
Take me to you.
Carry me to you.

Chorus
Carry me to you ...

But where the shadows fall
In the night of no recall
I'm waiting for you.
Waiting patiently for you.

Rowing boats ferry people across the Lagan on their way from the Ormeau Park.

ROLLING ON A TRAIN

This old town's been mean to me
I decided to break free
And get myself on the road.
Sold the house and the car
Had my last drink at the bar
And now I am getting on the train.

Chorus

That's why I'm rolling
Rolling on a train
Rolling. Rolling on a train
And I ain't coming back again.

My job was cheap, the pay was mean
I didn't like that working scene.
Too many ways to get put down.
Too many rules made by fools
I could never dance on cue
And so I had to quit town.

Repeat Chorus

My social life was getting me down
Too many drinks in the bars down town
I felt that I was going down the drain.
The people I knew were making me blue
A tired old case of *dé jà vu*
I just had to get away.

Repeat Chorus

I'm on a train to Dublin town
Engine wheels go round and round
Green fields forever goodbye.
In the morning breeze I'll be on the sea
On a ship called Liberty
And to America I'm bound.

Repeat Chorus

20

THE TITANIC

Year of nineteen-hundred-and-twelve
April the fourteenth day
The *Titanic* hit that berg
And the people all run and play
God knows, I know
God knows and the people all run and play.

The guards who had been watching
They thought they were fine
When they heard the great excitement
Many gunshots were fired
God knows etc.

Captain Smith gave orders
Women and children first
Manning the lifeboats oh la la
Many's a life was crushed
God knows etc.

Many had left their happy homes
And all that they possessed
Oh Jesus won't you hear us now?
Help us in our distress
God knows etc.

Women that left their loving ones
Feared for their safety when they heard their loved
ones doomed
Their hearts would almost break
God knows etc.

A.D.Smith mighty man
Built a boat that he didn't understand
Named it a name, God in a tin
Where is the sea God to hold it in?
God knows....

Traditional

POETRY

The Titanic *in Belfast Lough.*

DOWN ON THE DUBLIN TRAIN

Down on the Dublin train,
past Down's swift dips and hills,
almost seeing Narrow water, like a trailing ribbon
of sky, where I first dreamed your eyes and face

each and complete, dark and solemn,
heathery slopes reach to hold me,
tolerating no flower or bloom of colour
whispering beneath the ice:

she was once fair who walked this way,
but coldless and warmthless in the clay
she sleeps and never stirs
when winds moan strange among the firs.

She who once smiled upon bright eyes
dull-less and lightless as stone she lies
yes, as a spark within the flint
she left and came without a hint
of sorrow,
or tomorrow
another will come, flower-garlanded
as are all those who are handed
life's gift with little thought
and yet the earth sleeps on and can't forget
that which she wrought -

PROTESTANT

At home they spoke
Evasively
Evoking images of a dark and violent place.
'The Black North'.
Echoes of a big drum
Throbbing its pulse
Through the month of July.

Protestants were stereotypes
Fear-drawn on smudged
Pages of history.
Hard hats
Hard hearts
Rich and lost forever.
Square towered churches;
No warmth of graven images
Nor incense lingering
Like the scented aftermath of prayer.

A change came in time.
Twilight bled the deep colours
From the stained glass windows.
I saw only the leaden outline of saints,
Pale and grey
Peering in from the dark.

Today I stand apart
Picking my way through
History's galleries of art;
Seeing among the brush strokes
Finger prints of decadent popes.

I feel the need
To protest my innocence.

HEARSAY

Landlady
On the Golden Mile
Hiding your hurt
Behind a practised smile.

At first it was hearsay;
Heads nodding;
The weekly huddle of women
In the chapel yard
More intensity than usual.

Later it was confirmed.
One column inch
In the local Democrat
Discreetly whispered
Euphemistically
'A domestic tragedy -
A woman is helping the police
With their enquiries'.

Dinner was wasted -
Picked through, not tasted -
Minds cogitating the news.
Preoccupation was a veil
Rent at intervals
By exclamations
Beginning and ending
In silence.
'You would never have thought...'
'Her poor mother...'
'It'll be the talk of the country..'
'Never hear the last of it...'

We were cautioned
Charged 'not to say a word'.
The fact that it was common knowledge
Never entered the equation.
A conspiracy of silence
Suspended belief.

What was always known
Assumed a twisted history.
Had we ever envied
The glossy car
Her children's far away accents
Strange vowels
Shaped in the distant city?

At home in the plain kitchen
My father's fiddle sang
To his dancing touch;
His closed eyes savouring
The sound.
'Nan bought it for me;
Five pounds in Belfast
In ninteen-forty-three.'
Mother's flat voice
Dispelled the magic.
Was there a touch of envy
In her perfect recall
Her de-mythologising
Her narrative of small
Down-at-heel beginnings?

The Linen Hall. The City Hall now stands on this site.

'They were that poor
Nan's mother walked the roads
Begging charity.
A child of four
Numbed by barbed
Reminders of her poverty.
She came up the hard way
Fled to a servant's wage
Climbed by slow steps
To little dignities.

Landlady
On the Golden Mile
Hiding your hurt
Behind a practised smile.

After hours.
The sickening silence;
The tense waiting
For the first fist-fall.
Recurring nightmare
Of the bruised road
Travelled from poverty.

When the talk died down
You braved the whispering
From half-closed doors.
Some cried 'shameless'
Others said 'blameless'
You said: I was his wife.
It took a life to save a life,
Nothing more.
Remember
I have died before.

LOCH CRILLAN

I dteach i Loch Crillan théigh mé ballaí aoil challógach. I
bhfad uaim sheas na Cruacha Gorma stuama, liath-

Belfast from Castlereagh

chorcra. Ghluais taiséadach luaineach a sníodh ón cheo, thar chnoic nár ghéill do thuillte ama. I gciúnas reoite righin coiméadann siad síor-thonnaí na deoraíochta ag trá.

Stan mé ar thírdhreach a bhítréighte le fada. Cuibhrinn breac ag tithe a bhí teolaí uair.

Ruaig beirt fhear a raibh a n-óige caillte acu, an t-allas le muncillí sean-léinte gheala an Domhnaigh. Bhronn luascadh a speile máistreach an talaimh bhoicht orthu. Bhí páiste aonair a bhí ag súgradh lnena dtaobh, mar scáth ag a gcuis oibre. Bhí sí ag gabháil cheoil mar thionlachán ag siosarnach an fhéir ag casadh agus ag titim faoi chuaifeach na spéire.

Tháinig boladh tine mhóna chugam go milis agus láidir. Shnag an chumhra tréan mé. D'iompair sí cogarnach na nglúnta a d'imigh agus fonn eadrom teanga ársa Loch Chrillan.

THE TOWNLAND OF LOUGH CRILLAN

I warmed the flaking white-washed walls of a cottage in the townland of Lough Crillan. The Bluestack Mountains, purple-grey, stood solemn in the distance. Shifting shrouds weaved from mist, moved on mountains which resist, the surge of time. In stony, stolid silence they have watched the endless, exiled waves wash out from the land.

I gazed on a landscape that had long grown forlorn. Stone-walled fields speckled with the ruins of homes that once were warm. Two men whose youth had gone, wiped their sweat with the sleeves of old white Sunday shirts. The sway of scythes made them masters of impoverished soil. At their side, a solitary child played, shadow to toil. She sang along to the swish of hay, turning and tumbling against swirling sky.

Amid turf-fire smoke, sweet and strong, voices, generations gone — lingering tones of the old tongue in the townland of Lough Crillan.

THE HALF-DAY
BELFAST *CIRCA* 1972

Wednesdays inert in afternoons
with bearded Asiatic gentlemen, turbaned,
in their little grey Morris Minor vans.

Wednesday afternoons lean against street corners
in faded denims, or sprawl in the gutter
in Chapel Lane with a duncher at their
feet.

Wednesday afternoons stroll down the street,
released, like the souls of shop assistants,
at half-past one to gaze at jasperware
between the strands of Sellotape
on the plate-glass windows.

No two afternoons alike,
they jostle shoulders down Royal Avenue,
vacant eyed and eyeless,
stretched between noon and tea-time,
broken about four o'clock
for another chance to future gaze.

Tonight I folded this afternoon up,
tidily, along with my trousers and shirt.
Perhaps I'll wear it in the morning;
I don't know.

Evening and dusk and gloaming, darkling,
folded between half-closed lids,
crushed between mouth and hand
bitten to the quick:
a red sky in the evening,
a half-moon in the fingernail.

The Morning Star Bar, Pottinger's Entry.